© 2021 Chelsea Kong

All rights reserved. All images used in this book are licensed copies from their respectful owners including Freepik, Pixabay, Pexels, Unsplash, etc. This book or any portion thereof may not be reproduced or used in any manner whatsoever without the express written permission of the publisher except for the use of brief quotations in a book review.

Printed in 2021, Made in Toronto, Canada
ISBN: 978-1-990399-06-0
Library and Archives Canada

Jesus wants us to know Him.

He wants to share everything with us.

He wants us to be with Him forever.

LIVING WITH ABUNDANCE

Pray to Him every day and enjoy the unseen things.

Worship Him like David, praise, dance, and rest in Him.

# What can we do?

Listen to Jesus and do what He says.

Use your gifts to share your love for Him.

Pray for others to know Him.

Obey your parents and those God puts over your life.

# Take time to do these

Go to church every week

Give to others and you will be blessed.

Return your tithes and give offerings.

Help the poor and needy.

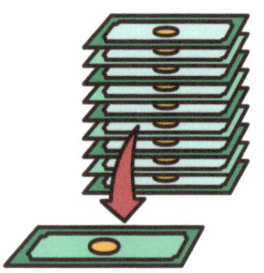

# Spend time with Him

Jesus wants us to make time for Him.

You can ask Him about anything.

Take time to enjoy Him and His presence.

You need to do this every day like Mary sat at His feet.

# Know God's Word

Read God's Word every day.

Ask the Holy Spirit to teach us God's Word.

Make time to do this.

It is better to do it in the morning and before you sleep.

# Pray Every Day

Daniel prayed three times a day.

Ask, Seek, and Knock.

Believe that God heard you and that you already have it.

Speak God's Word when you pray.

# Come in Faith

Jesus likes it when we believe Him.

Know that He loves you.

Trust Him all the time.

Give Him your whole heart.

# Listen and do

Let Jesus talk to you as long as He wants.

Draw, write, speak, dance, sing, and more.

Follow what He tells you.

Be happy when you do it.

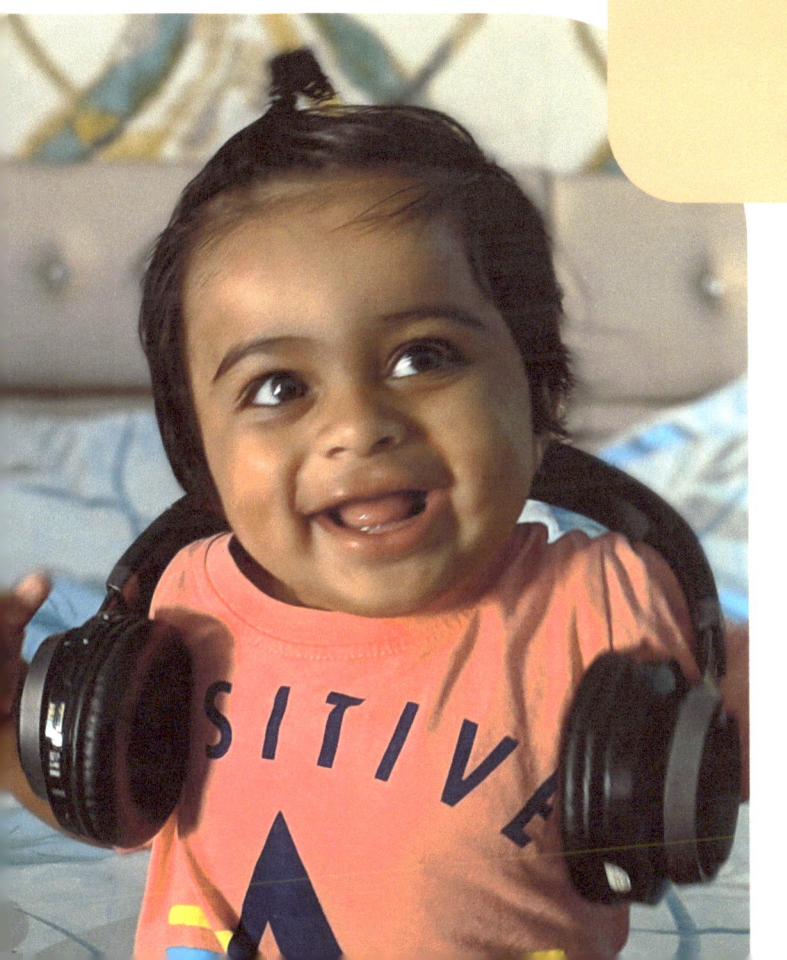

# Love Others

Help others to know what God's Word says.

You can spend time with them and use our gifts.

Give them money, gifts, or other things.

Pray for them and share Jesus with them.

# Honour Him as King

Jesus is our King and wants our love and respect.

Give Him our best.

Worship Him, give thanks, and praise to Him.

Let Jesus ask us what we want.

# Let Jesus help us

Jesus will answer us and deal with our enemies.

He is with us all the time.

He will give us His best.

He gives us rewards when we obey Him.

# Jesus Prays for us

Jesus wants us to know Him.

He wants to share everything with us.

He wants us to be with Him forever.

# Jesus Heart

He shares secrets with us.

He tells and shows us things.

He loves people and wants to save them.

He tells you what to pray for and gives you ideas.

# Fasting and Prayer

Jesus fasted 40 days and nights.

He became strong and close to God.

No food and water and lots of time praying.

Holy Spirit gave Him power and strength.

# Be sensitive

Jesus obeyed God always.

He worked with the Holy Spirit.

He did not sin.

He knew God's voice and the Holy Spirit.

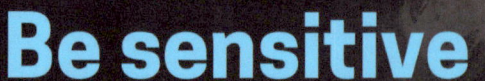

# Supernatural

Jesus turned water into wine.

He walked on water.

He healed the sick set people free.

He raised Lazarus from the dead.

# Taught the Disciples

He told them about God and His Kingdom.

He taught them how to do miracles.

Jesus taught the disciples the Lord's prayer.

He showed them who He is and how to pray God's Word.

# Jesus Tempted and Tested

Jesus was tempted when he had no food and water.

He was tested when Peter was tempted.

He was tempted in the Garden of Gethsemane.

A soldier gave him vinegar water.

# His Betrayal

He knows how we feel when people hurt us.

Judas sold Jesus for money, but Jesus knew about it.

He warned His disciples what will happen.

He was alone when his enemies took Him.

# His Death and Salvation

Jesus died for us to save us.

The cross shows how much He loves us.

He gave us freedom through His blood.

He gave us the long-lasting life and more than what we need.

# The Promise

He said He will give us the Holy Spirit.

We need to wait for the answer.

God will do it in His perfect time.

Grow in your faith to want His will done.

# A New Life

Live for Jesus every day.

Stay close to Him and be holy.

Watch your heart and the words you speak.

Give yourself to Him fully.

# Jesus as Savior

He is the one who saved us from sin.

Jesus wants to save everyone.

Believe and accept Him as your Savior and Lord.

He comes into our heart to live inside us.

# Jesus Resurrection

Jesus rose from the grave after three days.

He went to heaven and lives there with God.

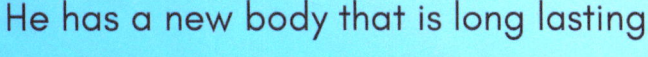

He has a new body that is long lasting.

Jesus pleased God.

# Jesus Knows

He knows our heart and mind.

Stay away from evil and always forgive.

Live a life that pleases Him.

Be aware of what people say and do.

# Always pray

We need to always pray.

Keep watch and pray.

Ask what to pray.

Speak out Psalm 91 and the Armour of God every day.

# Jesus as Lord

We need to let Jesus be the first place in our life.

He is control of our life, so give Him everything.

It means we must do what He says all the time.

He has the highest position.

# Holy Communion

We need to let Jesus be the first place in our life.

He is control of our life, so give Him everything.

It means we must do what He says all the time.

He has the highest position.

# Jesus as our Groom and King

Jesus is our Groom and we are His Bride.

He wants us to be clean and holy.

We must fear God and be ready for Jesus' return.

Commit to Him and allow Him to change you.

# Jesus is coming back

Jesus will come back for His Bride: The Church.

He wants us to be always ready for Him.

We need to always share Jesus with everyone.

We do not know when He will come back.

# Final Words

We need to follow Jesus in how we talk and live our life.

Those who have Jesus in their life are saved.

Jesus will judge those who don't know Him.

Do God's work all the time and want only Him.

# SALVATION PRAYER

God, I know I sinned against you. Forgive me for the wrong that I have done. I believe that Jesus Christ died on the cross for me. That He rose from the grave so that after three days. I can have His long-lasting life. Come into my heart to be my Lord and Savior. I choose to turn away from my sins and I choose to follow you. Lead me to walk with you. Keep me safe and teach me your ways. Stop every bad thing in my life that has an open door to hurt me. Close those doors. Holy Spirit fill me now in Jesus' name. Amen.

# BAPTISM IN THE HOLY SPIRIT

Jesus, you are the one that fills me with Your Spirit. Come Holy Spirit and come into my life and fill me to overflow with Your presence. Come with your fire too. Thank you for the gift of tongues in Jesus' name. Amen.

Open your mouth and let the words come out that God gives you. It will be words that you don't know what they mean. You can ask God what it means. You need to let Him talk through you every day to grow this gift.

He will bring you closer to God and you will know Jesus more. You will have power from God to do great things and know things.

# PRAYER

Jesus, teach how to follow you and how to love. Give me a heart to share with others. Help me to stay close to you. To speak the right words and do what pleases you. That I hear you all the time. Show me how to live in your presence. I want to know you more. Teach me how to follow the Holy Spirit. I give my life fully to you in Jesus' name. Amen.

# Message from the Author

Jesus said that He came to give us life and life more abundantly. This means to have more than what we need. It is to give more to others. He wants us to always have more. His Word is important for our life to be blessed. It is the only way for people to know Him. We need to stay strong in Him. The enemy will fight hard to keep us from Jesus. Holy Spirit lives inside us when we have Jesus in our heart. His power comes only after we have the gift of the Holy Spirit. He will help us.

# OTHER PRODUCTS

- Knowing God
- How to Hear God's Voice
- New Life in Jesus
- Loving Israel
- God's Gifts
- Meeting God
- Word Power
- Fruit of the Spirit
- The Tabernacle
- Bride for Jesus
- A Life of Prayer
- Live Free
- Who am I in Jesus
- Walk in Love
- God's Favor
- Man of God
- Woman of God
- How to Use Money
- God's Wisdom
- Fasting
- See Jerusalem and Bethany
- First Fruit Offering
- Feast of Trumpets
- Day of Atonement
- Feast of Tabernacles
- Counting the Omer
- Festival of Lights
- Glory, Presence, and Holy Spirit
- Live in God's Presence
- Pentecost
- 31 Day Devotional
- Biblical Puzzle Book Vol 1
- Biblical Puzzle Book Vol 2
- Biblical Puzzle Book Vol 3
- Biblical Puzzle Book Vol 4
- Biblical Puzzle Book Vol 5
- Bible Puzzles for Young Children Book 1
- Bible Puzzles for Young Children Book 2
- Bible Puzzles for Young Children Book 3
- Biblical Puzzle for Children Books 1-3
- How God Speaks
- Knowing Jesus
- Knowing Holy Spirit

# OTHER PRODUCTS

**Teaching Series**
How to Hear God's Voice Teaching Guide & Audio Book
Relationship with God, Jesus, Holy Spirit Guide
Knowing God, Jesus, Holy Spirit Guide & Audio Book

**Teaching (Non-Sale on my website)**
Purim
Passover
Resurrection

More books to come!

More books on Amazon, Kobo, and Barnes and Noble
https://chelseak532002550.wordpress.com/

More books on Amazon, Kobo, and Barnes and Noble
https://www.amazon.com/author/chelseakong

Please leave a review and share with friends to help the author continue to write more books to reach more readers. Thank you so much for your support.

# About
## CHELSEA KONG

She is a writer, creative arts and digital media artist, skilled administration professional, and podcaster. Chelsea also served in a variety of roles, from audiovisual, photography, to assisting on the worship team, and ministry team. She also has a passion for families being united.

Chelsea has been a guest on Unity Live Radio and The Lady Tracey Show and is highly recommended by a Proud Christian blog. She graduated from Hotel and Restaurant Management, Digital Media Arts, Office Administration, and experience working with children. Chelsea lives in Toronto, Canada. She mainly writes children's books, stories, bridal writing, poems, lyrics for songs, words of encouragement, blessings, prayers, and jokes. The author of How to Hear the Voice of God, the Bridal Collection, Knowing God, etc. She also has her own Bible Puzzle books and other inspired products. Her podcast channel is called Chelsea K on Anchor, Spotify, and iTunes.

Please check my website to find out more:
https://chelseak532002550.wordpress.com/

www.ingramcontent.com/pod-product-compliance
Lightning Source LLC
Chambersburg PA
CBHW041413010526
44107CB00016B/1158